PARIS, FRANCE

Travel Guide Book

A Comprehensive 5-Day Travel Guide to Paris, France
& Unforgettable French Travel

• Travel Guides to Europe Series •

Passport to European Travel Guides

☯

Eye on Life Publications

Paris, France Travel Guide Book
Copyright © 2015 Passport to European Travel Guides

ISBN 10: 151479859X
ISBN 13: 978-1514798591

~

All rights reserved. No part of this book may be reproduced in any form or by any electronic or mechanical means, including information storage and retrieval systems, without permission in writing from the publisher, except by a reviewer who may quote brief passages in a review. All photos used courtesy of freeimages.com, HAAP Media Ltd., a subsidiary of Getty Images.

Other Travel Guide Books by
Passport to European Travel Guides

Provence & the French Riviera, France

London, England

Santorini, Greece

Barcelona, Spain

Istanbul, Turkey

Prague, Czech Republic

Rome, Italy

Venice, Italy

Florence, Italy

Naples & the Amalfi Coast, Italy

"We'll always have Paris."
—Rick Blaine, Casablanca (1942)

Table of Contents

Map of Paris, France..0
Introduction: How to Use this Guide..................................1
City Snapshot..2
Before You Go..3
Getting in the Mood..8
    • What to Read?...8
    • What to Watch?..8
Local Tourist Information..9
About the Airports...9
How Long is the Flight?...10
Overview of Paris, France...11
★ Insider Tips For Tourists! ★......................................13
French Phrases For Emergencies......................................21
Climate and Best Times to Travel....................................26
Tours...30
    • By Bike..30
    • By Boat..31
    • By Bus...31
    • By Minibus or Car..32
    • Special-Interest and Walking Tours...........................32
★ 5-Day Guide to Paris ★ Itinerary! ★...............................34
    • Day 1..34
    • Day 2..35
    • Day 3..36
    • Day 4..37

- Day 5 38
- Best Places For Travelers on a Budget 39
  - Bargain Sleeps 39
  - Bargain Eats 41
- Best Spots For Ultimate Luxury 43
  - Luxury Parisian Sleeps 43
  - Luxury Parisian Eats 44
- Paris Nightlife 45
  - Great Bars in Paris 45
  - Great Clubs in Paris 46
  - Great Live Music in Paris 46
  - Great Theatre in Paris 47
  - Great Music and Dance 48
- Conclusion 49
- About the Authors 50

Map of Paris, France

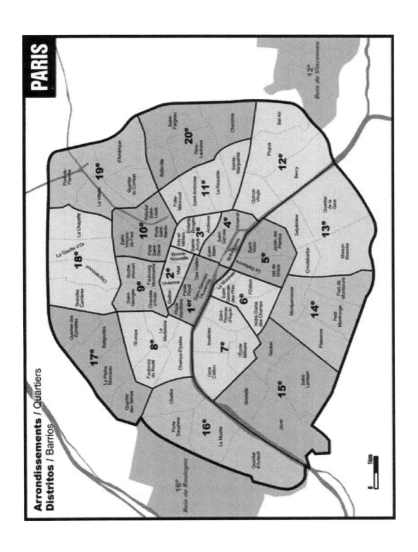

• Introduction •

Paris, France. The "City of Love." The "City of Lights." It's most definitely one of the most beautiful cosmopolitan cities in the entire world! You can't possibly plan to travel through Europe without having *Paris* on your itinerary, right?

Although the city's quite vast and everyone speaks French — never fear! There's absolutely no need to be even *remotely* intimidated, because you've picked up the most comprehensive travel guide there is, and we've got you covered!

In this 5-day guide to Paris, France, you'll get the sharpest recommendations and **tips** to best prepare you with everything you need to know in order to have a most successful and memorable Parisian experience!

Be sure to read over the **insider tips** carefully and familiarize yourself with the information so you can pack and prepare accordingly. Every traveler is different, so we've included a variety of information and recommendations to suit all interests.

You can plan according to our detailed **5-day itinerary,** or you can mix it up and **mix and match your activities** and scheduling. We encourage you to do whatever works for the enjoyment of your trip!

Enjoy!

The Passport to European Travel Guides Team

• City Snapshot •

Language: French

Local Airports: Paris Charles de Gaulle Airport | Orly Airport

Currency: Euro (€)

Country Code: 33

Emergencies: Dial 112 (for any emergency within the European Union), 17 (police), 18 (fire department), 15 (first aid, EMS). The emergency calls at 112 are answered in Italian, English, French, and German.

Arrondissement? It means district.

• Before You Go... •

✓ Have a Passport

If you don't already have one, you'll need to **apply for a passport** in your home country a good two months before you intend to travel, to avoid cutting it too close. You'll need to find a local passport agency, complete an application, take fresh photos of yourself, have at least one form of ID and pay an application fee. If you're in a hurry, you can usually expedite the application for a 2-3 week turnaround at an additional cost.

✓ Need a Visa?

Residents of the US, Mexico and many other countries don't need to apply for a French visa unless they plan to stay in France for longer than **three months**. However, citizens of some countries (such as China) need to apply for a visa no matter how long they plan to stay. If you're unsure, just **check with your local consulate**.

The US State Department provides a wealth of country-specific information for American travelers, including **travel alerts and warnings**, the location of the **US embassy in each country**, and of course, **whether or not you need a visa** to travel there! http://travel.state.gov/content/passports/english/country.html

✓ Healthcare

Most people neglect this, but it's important to keep in mind when traveling to any foreign country. It's wise to **consult with your doctor** about your travel plans and ensure **routine immunizations are current**. You want to protect against things like influenza, polio, chickenpox, mumps, measles, etc.

And although France's medical system is nationalized and visitor-friendly, it's still advisable to **ensure you'll be covered** when you travel abroad.

✓ Set the Date

Choose the **best time for the best experience!** Unless you have no aversion to high expenses and/or heat, it's best to travel to Paris in the **off-season** — meaning avoid the holidays and the summertime (although the longer days in June give more time for **sightseeing and relaxing in cafés!**). Book flights, hotels and train passes **as far in advance** as possible, and you'll get better rates all around.

✓ Pack

- If you don't want to feel **underdressed** in comparison to the French, leave the denim shorts and tennis shoe-type clothing at home — they just scream "tourist!"

Opt for solid colors, slacks and dress shirts, scarves, skirts and dresses. Be sure to check the local weather in Paris for the time of year you're traveling and pack sweaters, jackets, or coats accordingly. It's always a good idea to **pack an umbrella or raincoat and clothes**

for layering in cooler weather, and a good pair of **walking shoes** that you'll be comfortable in.

• Pack well, but don't pack too much! Leave space for all the great shopping you'll be doing in Paris shops! Otherwise, you'll end up having to buy extra luggage and pay those ghastly baggage fees on the trip home.

• Be sure to pack a good **conversational French phrase guide** to bring along with you. You'll find people a lot friendlier toward you if you don't go around assuming they speak your language.

• **Hand sanitizer** is always great to have along with you when traveling.

• **Medication.** Don't forget to have enough for the duration of your trip. It's also helpful to have a **note from your physician** if you're concerned about being questioned about carrying a certain quantity.

• Bring one or two **reusable shopping bags** for trips to the grocery store and for carrying souvenirs home.

• Travelers from outside Europe will need to bring along a **universal electrical plug converter** that can work for both lower and higher voltages. This way you'll be able to plug in your cell phones, tablets, curling irons, etc., during the trip.

• Be sure to **leave expensive jewels and high-priced electronics at home**. Like most major cities and tourist attractions, thieves and pickpockets abound. Avoid making yourself a target.

✓ Phone Home

How will you call home from France? Does your cell phone company offer service while abroad? What are their rates? Other options are to **buy a French phone chip** for your phone — which also gives you a French phone number — buy calling codes in your home country, or you can **buy calling cards** when you arrive in Paris.

✓ Currency Exchange

The currency in France is the euro so you'll need to exchange your $ for €. It's a good idea to have **at most 200 euros** to pay for transportation, tipping, and any other travel expense you may incur.

France is considered one of the more expensive countries to visit, so it's good to be prepared. ATMs are readily available and you'll get the exchange rate on the day of withdrawal. Unless it can't be avoided, **never carry more than 200 euros** in cash on you at a time; this will minimize your losses in the event of theft.

It's no longer the days of Charles Dickens, but Paris still has its **fair share of pickpockets**.

Make sure your bank knows you'll be traveling abroad. This way you avoid having foreign country transactions flagged and declined, which can be extremely inconvenient.

✓ Contact Your Embassy

In the unfortunate event you should lose your passport or be victimized while in France, **your country's embassy** will be able to help you. Be sure to give your itinerary and contact information to a **close friend or family member**, then also contact your embassy with your emergency contact information before you leave home.

✓ Your Mail

Ask a neighbor to check your mailbox while you're away, or visit your local post office and request a hold. **Overflowing mailboxes** are a dead giveaway that no one's home.

• Getting in the Mood •

Here are a few great **books and films** set in Paris that we recommend you watch in preparation for your trip to this magical city!

What to Read:

The Sweet Life in Paris: Delicious Adventures in the World's Most Glorious and Perplexing City by David Lebovitz Join David on his move to Paris and humorous journey to falling in love with the amazingly eclectic city!

Almost French: Love and a New Life in Paris by Sarah Turnbull A super sweet story of finding love and a whole new life in Paris!

Anna and the French Kiss by Stephanie Perkins Will Anna be French kissed? You'll have to read it to find out!

What to Watch:

Sabrina (1995) A sensitive young woman's journey from the north shore of Long Island to the heart of Paris! Julia Ormond and Harrison Ford shine in these performances!

Julie & Julia (2009) Bon appétit — with Amy Adams and Meryl Streep!

Last Tango in Paris (1972) A scintillating and sensuous ride with the great Marlon Brando against the backdrop of...you guessed it — Paris!

Enjoy!

• Local Tourist Information •

As soon as you arrive at either Charles de Gaulle (CDG) or Orly (ORY) airport, you can get brochures, maps and other helpful information from the regional tourism board. There are lots of kiosks.

The main civic **tourist information office** is centrally located on Rue des Pyramides (near the Opéra). Four other branches are conveniently located at the most popular tourist spots. While most are open daily, the Gare de Lyon and Gare de L'Est branches, are only open Monday through Saturday.

The tourist bureaus have helpful and friendly multilingual staff ready to provide you with information about local transportation, hotels, apartments, getaways, discount passes and current special events taking place in the city.

You can buy museum passes and the highly sought after Versailles passports to save on time. During summertime, there are additional kiosks near areas like the Champs-Élysées, Notre-Dame, Bastille and Hotel de Ville.

• About the Airports •

Charles de Gaulle (also known as Roissy) is 16 miles (26 km) northeast of Paris. Orly Airport is 10 miles

(16 km) south of Paris. Both are easy to get to from the city.

Give yourself an extra hour or two to make your way through the airport, especially in the peak travel seasons. Traffic is quite dense near both.

• How Long is the Flight? •

- **From New York** to Paris = approx. 7 hours
- **From Miami** = approx. 9 hours
- **From Chicago** = approx. 8 hours
- **From Los Angeles** = approx. 11 hours
- **From London** = approx. 1.5 hours
- **From Sydney** = approx. 21.5 hours
- **From Cape Town** = approx. 14 hours

Security is taken very seriously in France, so be prepared for long lines at checkpoints. And never leave your bags or belongings unattended. Unattended items are considered a security risk and could be destroyed.

You may see no shortage of armed security officers patrolling both airports.

• Overview of Paris, France •

With more than 12 million residents, Paris is home to about 19% of France's total population. The very multicultural, cosmopolitan city that thrives today is a far cry from the ancient Paris that started its life after a war between Celtics and Romans, and as a rather tiny community.

With a long and enduring history, amazing architecture — from the baroque and medieval periods to the present day — a diverse society that offers great music, art and theatre, numerous sporting opportunities and a range of high cuisine, Paris calls out to us all. The city offers a great, yet diverse, lifestyle for its residents, but a mesmerizing time for those who visit, if only for the weekend. **It's always magical.**

From the many amazing parks to the amazing architecture to the designer fashions, Paris is never short on things to do.

Nowadays Paris is among the great cities of the world, a must-visit destination for bucket lists and random travel adventures alike. It's also multiple visit-friendly, as different times of year in Paris offer different and unique charms.

For instance, in the springtime the locals come out in large numbers, taking their coffee at pavement cafes, strolling or jogging in lush parks, like the Jardin des Tuileries or Jardin du Luxembourg. In the summertime while visitors pour in, in large numbers, many Parisians are off on holiday to homes by the sea.

In autumn, the parks get a subtle shade of gold, while winter in this lovely city offers its crisp, frosty mornings, a stunning sight guaranteed to stay with you, should you dare to brave a winter in the city of lights.

• Insider Tips For Tourists •

As you can imagine, Paris usually fills up at peak times. Therefore, if it's at all possible, avoid the weekends and school holiday times in summer.

If you love **museums**, then you ought to visit in the **first weekend** of the month when admissions and top sites are **totally free!**

Hotels in Paris usually don't include breakfast in their rates, but the hotel breakfast (buffet-style) can be economical.

Single hotel rooms usually cost the same as a double room.

Build your itinerary properly so as to maximize on the discounts you could be eligible for, i.e. citizens of EU who are under the age of 26 years are eligible for free admission at monuments and national museums, which include Sainte Chapelle, the Louvre, Musee d'Orsay, Musee Rodin and Musee Picasso.

Etiquette

The French really don't deserve their infamous reputation for being rude. Parisians in particular are sticklers for sophistication and formality, and American-style manners are considered informal and impolite.

The first thing you should ask when engaging someone is: "Do you speak English?" That's sure to get you off on better footing than initially approaching someone *in English*...and even better if you actually **say it in French:** "Parlez-vous Anglais?" (parlay-voo onglay?)

Before you go, or during your flight, etc, take the time to learn a few common French words and phrases you'll need for interacting with shop attendants, street vendors, etc.

Always greet with **bonjour** (bohn-jhoor), which means "Hello" or "Good day," when you go into a hotel, store, shop or café; and *au revoir* (orhuv-whar) "Goodbye" whenever you leave, no matter who seems to be paying attention to you. Sometimes only a few people will respond, while at other times everyone will!

When addressing a female who's over the age of 16 use *madame* (ma-dam), which means, "My lady." For younger girls, use *mademoiselle* (mad-mwa-zel), which means "miss."

It's *monsieur* (muh-syur) for both boys and men alike.

Be sure you always say please, *s'il vous plaît* (see-voo-play), and thank you, *merci* (mehr-see).

Time Zone

There's a six-hour time difference between New York and Paris. Paris is ahead on the clock. When it's 8AM in New York, it's 2PM in Paris).

The time difference between London, England and Paris, France is one hour, with Paris being ahead. (8AM in London is 9AM in Paris).

The format for abbreviating dates in Europe is different from the US. They use: day/month/year, so 6/9/15 means September 6, 2015 to Europeans.

Saving Time & Money

Since Paris is one of the world's most visited (and crowded) cities, you're likely to have a better experience if you make certain preparations well in advance. Whenever possible, buy tickets for just about everything online: most of the museums and cultural centers sell tickets in advance. There may be a minimal service fee but it's well worth it to avoid spending all your time waiting in lines.

Look into alternative entrances at the more popular tourist sites (for example, the Louvre has three); check for reduced rates, which are mostly once a week when they're open late. Also, as mentioned earlier, on the **first Sunday of every month**, national museums, including the Louvre (http://www.louvre.fr/en), Centre Pompidou (https://www.centrepompidou.fr/en) and Musée d'Orsay (http://www.musee-orsay.fr/) are actually **free of charge!**

If you're really interested in sightseeing, it's a good idea to buy a Museum Pass to save money and also to bypass waiting in lines. They're sold at the airports, the major métro stations, the tourism office in the Carrousel du Louvre, and at each destination the pass covers. (http://www.parismuseumpass.com)

As of early 2015, two-day pass cost €42; four-day pass are €56; six-day pass are €69.

Use ATMs for the **best exchange rates**, they're everywhere; buying euros at your hotel or in a store will almost always cost you more.

Tipping

By law, bills in restaurants and bars must include service (some servers may tell you otherwise but don't believe them), so you **do not** have to tip, however it is polite to round your bill up a couple euros if you're happy with the service. **Use your discretion** — for a beer you may leave an extra €0.25, for a meal you might leave €1–€3.

In high-end restaurants (such as those we recommend later in this guide) it's customary to leave a 5% tip on the table.

Tip **taxi drivers and hairdressers** 10% of the bill.

After **lengthy road trips,** you should tip the bus driver about €2.

After **guided tours,** tip the guide about 10% of the price of the tour.

Watch out for signs that say *pourboire interdit* — tipping banned/forbidden; otherwise you can tip theater and hotel cloakroom attendants €0.50, but they usually expect nothing.

If you're in a hotel for more than two or three days, leave about €1–€2 per day for the maid. It's appropriate to tip €2 (€1 in a moderately priced hotel) to whoever carries your bags or hails your taxi. **For room service**, give €1–€2 to the server (with the exception of routine breakfast).

If the maid does **pressing or laundering** for you, tip her €1.50–€2.

If the **concierge** was helpful, leave a tip of €5–€15, at your own discretion.

When You Have to Go

Public toilets in Paris are typically unisex, so be prepared to share. You'll also need to buy something as a customer if you want to use the restroom in a café, bar or shop.

There are about 400 *sanisettes*, free public toilet units, all around the city. Are they clean? Well, they self-clean after each use so they'll be as clean as can be expected.

Department stores, fast-food chains and public parks are all good places to find **clean** public toilets.

Train, metro stations, upscale clubs and restaurants often have restroom attendants who keep them clean, so it's a good idea to have change on you when using these facilities.

Although they've become scarce, it's possible to run into **Turkish-style toilets** — a mere hole in the ground. **When you flush these**, step as far away as you can to avoid having the water splash your shoes or clothes.

Sometimes the light in a bathroom comes on only once the cubicle door is closed and locked. They often work on a timer to save on electricity, 3 minutes tops.

So if the light goes off before you're finished, simply press the button again.

Taxes

By law, affixed prices in France must include taxes. Restaurants and hotels must include all service charges and taxes in their prices. If you ever see these as additional charges on a bill, do not pay it before addressing it with a manager.

There is one exception, with hotels and other lodging accommodations: you may see a tourist tax or *taxe de séjour* added to your bill at checkout time that can range anywhere from €0.20 to €1.50 per person, per day.

V.A.T.—Value-Added Tax is known in France as *taxe sur la valeur ajoutée,* or TVA. As of this writing, the standard rate is 20%. **Luxury goods** are taxed up to 33%; food in restaurants 10%. TVA tax for services is not refundable, but foreigners can get a TVA refund on products and goods. The item/s must be purchased for €175.01 on a single day in a participating shop (watch for the 'Tax-Free' notice on the door or window).

Obtain VAT refunds through the PABLO system. Here's how it works: Retailers that participate will give you a computer-generated PABLO V.A.T. refund form with a barcode. When you get to the airport, **before you check-in your luggage,** you need to scan your barcode at a PABLO machine to get the refund credited to your bank account. Service is provided in English.

 The most common European V.A.T. refund system is **Global Blue**. Watch for their sign when shopping. Their service provides refunds in a variety of options: credit card adjustment, check or cash.

Phone Calls

The country code for France is 33. When calling into France from outside the country, you drop the first 0 from the number. For example, the number for the Notre-Dame Cathedral is 1-42-34-56-10. To call this number from Miami, you would dial 00-33-1-42-34-56-10. **But to call from within Paris**, you dial 01-42-34-56-10.

When calling home from Paris, first dial 00 after which you'll hear a tone. Then dial the country code (1 for the US and Canada, 44 for the UK, 61 for Australia and 64 for New Zealand, 52 for Mexico, 7 for Russia, 86 for China, 81 for Japan), then the area code without the initial 0, then the number.

It's often expensive to call internationally, especially if you do so from a hotel phone. They almost always add surcharges.

Buying **local calling cards** can keep staying in touch less of an expense.

Prepaid cell phones can be bought in Paris at a rate of about €0.70/minute to call the US or Canada. Depending on the provider, the rest of the world can be nearly double. Incoming calls are usually free.

If you decide to **bring your own cell phone**, check with your provider on coverage and rates. Texting internationally tends to be less expensive.

Most landlines in France include service plans that cover international calls, but it's a good idea to verify this before making calls if you're renting an apartment.

If you want to **reach an operator** for help placing a call, **dial 08-00-99-00** (toll free) together with the last two digits of the country's code. So for help calling the US and Canada from Paris, you would dial 08-00-99-00-11. For England you would dial: 08-00-99-00-44. For Mexico you would dial 08-00-99-00-52.

Electricity

Paris' electrical current is 220 volts. As discussed before, when traveling from outside of Europe you will need to bring an adapter and converter that enable you to plug your electronics and appliances into the sockets they use. Cell phone, tablet and laptop chargers are typically dual voltage, so you won't need a converter, just an adapter to be able to plug it in.

Most small appliances are likely to be dual voltage, but **always double check** when possible, especially with hair dryers and travel irons.

In Emergencies

Don't pick up the phone in Paris and dial 911. It won't work. In France, the numbers for emergencies are as follows:

Dial 112 — police, fire, or ambulance

Dial 15 — medical emergencies

Dial 17 — police department

Dial 18 — fire department

French Phrases For Emergencies:

"poste de police" (police station)

"médecin" (doctor)

"urgence" (emergency)

"hôpital" (hospital)

"pompiers" (firemen)

"au secours!" (help!)

The city is set up very efficiently to handle emergencies with fully staffed hospitals within 30 minutes of all Parisian residents. ER wait times for walk-ins can be lengthy, but typically not as long as they can be in the United States.

Your hotel or nearby pharmacy should be able to direct you to a local hospital, or primary doctor which can cost anywhere from €20-€40 + any medications you'll need at a pharmacy. Costs at public hospitals in the city, such as Hôpital Hôtel Dieu (which is next to Notre Dame Cathedral • Rue de la Cité, M° Cité, 4th • Phone: 01 42 34 82 32), are quite lower than at private hospitals in the suburbs.

However, should you get sick in the middle of the night or feel too ill to visit a physician, there is also another medical service in France you can use. **SOS Médécins** (phone: 01 47 07 77 77), for medical emergencies, and **SOS Dentaire** (phone: 01 43 37 51 00) for dental. **Within the hour** a certified (usually bi-lingual) physician will make a house call for about €65-€75, depending on your medication needs.

For minor issues, you can seek out a nearby pharmacy (la pharmacie) as they are able to recommend over-the-counter medications and licensed to administer first-aid. If they don't speak English, they can refer you to the nearest English-speaking pharmacy.

Holidays

France has eleven national holidays. In May, there's one almost every week and banks, museums and stores are closed. Also, when a holiday falls on a Tuesday or Thursday, you'll find that a lot of business go ahead and close on that Monday or Friday also.

Here are the holidays by month; dates are not included, as most fluctuate each year. Check for the specific dates during the year you're booking your trip to Paris and plan accordingly.

January 1 (New Year's Day)

April (Easter Weekend)

May (Labor Day)

May (VE Day)

May (Ascension Day)

June (Pentecost Monday)

July (Bastille Day)

August (Assumption)

November (All Saints' Day)

November (Armistice)

December 25 (Christmas Day)

Hours of Operation

Most of the **museums** in Paris are closed at least one day a week, typically Mondays and Tuesdays. They stay open late at least one night per week, and this is usually the least crowded time.

Bank hours are typically 9:00 am - 5:00 pm, but close for up to two hours at lunch. You can find some banks open on Saturday.

Supermarkets and groceries generally open at around 8:00 am and close around 8:00 pm. You can usually find a small corner store open until 11:00pm but prices are often higher.

Don't try to be an early bird for **shopping** in Paris. Most store hours are typically 9:30 am or 10:00 am to 7:00 or 8:00 pm. Some smaller shops don't open until 11:00 am, and then still close for a few hours at lunch. Many shops and stores along the Champs-Élysées and other tourist sites don't often open before 2:00 pm.

On Sundays, your best bet for shopping is department stores, as most shops are closed.

Government offices and businesses are usually 9:00 am - 5:00 pm.

Money

Traveling to Paris can be tough to do on a tight budget, but if you take the time to look, there are places you can go to avoid the tourist traps and save money.

Tourist areas will have higher pricing than any others. So don't expect to save money in boutiques, restaurants or hotels around, say, the Louvre or the Champs-Élysées areas.

You can find better prices in the Saint Michel/Sorbonne area in the Rive Gauche, the Bastille, Republique, Beleville areas in east Paris, Les Halles, Le Marais in the city center, and in the Montparnasse, south of the boulevard.

It's best to utilize **ATMs** and tellers in the **non-tourist areas** of the city and be sure to use common sense and not make yourself a target for pickpockets. If anyone approaches you unexpectedly, it's best to politely keep walking.

Also, **beware the unnecessary fees.** If you're given the option to pay in dollars vs. euros when using your credit card, simply say no. Paying in dollars **will cost you more** in fees and you may or may not be informed of the additional charges at the time of the transaction.

If you're on a budget, you can choose to eat at the counter in some restaurants and pay less. Cafés and bars also cost less at the counter. **You'll typically see two prices** on the menu: *au comptoir* (at counter) and *à salle* (at table) and *sur la terrasse* (on the terrace).

Many popular restaurants boutiques and shops have their menus and pricings on their websites. It's a good idea to check out prices and plan ahead if you're on a budget.

Climate and Best Times to Travel

When planning to visit Paris, the most pressing decision is often deciding the right time to visit.

The peak travel times are between the middle of July and September, late December to early January for the holiday season, and during the February school break.

Wintertime in general is mostly dark and cold, but if you're looking for low airfare and good hotel deals, it may be an ideal time to go.

April is usually the rainy season.

In June, the days are nice and long for exploring, sightseeing and enjoying outdoor cafés since sunset isn't until around 10 pm. However, **summer is the most crowded and costly** time to visit Paris.

Many people avoid going in **August**. Not only is it hot, but locals are on vacation, so many restaurants and cafes are closed. But there's still fun to be had in August—lots of free outdoor concerts, movies, and the "Paris Beaches," or Paris-Plages, along the River Seine.

Paris in September is gorgeous. Nice weather, reasonable airfares and lots of cultural events to enjoy. There's also the annual Journées du Patrimoine, or Patrimony Days, the third week in September, when many national buildings that are usually closed to the general public open up their doors.

Transportation

Most expensive? Taxi cabs. A ride to and from either of the airports can run you anywhere from €35-€70, depending on the time of day and distance to your destination.

Least expensive? Suburban express train, which runs about €9.50, including connection.

On arrival at Paris' Charles de Gaulle airport, you can take a **bus** to your destination, which is much less expensive than taking a cab, which again, is the most expensive mode of transportation you'll find.

The RATP bus 350 and RATP bus 351 are the most **cost effective** ways of getting to the heart of the city.

A company called **Roissybus** runs busses from various parts of Paris 24 hours a day every 15 minutes from 6 am to 8:45 pm, then every 20 minutes through 11 pm. The cost is €10 per person. The trip to the airport can take around 45 minutes in normal traffic and as long as 90 minutes during rush hour.

The **Metro** system is extensive, efficient and easy to use once you're used to it. You can just grab a map and hop on. They have automated systems that walk you through buying your tickets and you can chose to use them in English. **Wait times** are often less than five minutes.

Air France has a comfortable shuttle service you can also use to get to and from the city, and you don't have to be an Air France passenger to use it.

For folks with **lots of luggage** or children, there are also **van companies** like SuperShuttle Paris that serve both airports. Unlike cabs, fares are fixed price. Call or make a reservation online at least a week in advance, and a comfortable van with a bilingual driver can await your arrival and take you wherever you'd like to go. Be sure to **confirm your reservation** the day before you travel. Sometimes the van books more than one party so you may have to share with other passengers both ways.

Driving

As a tourist, it's best to **avoid driving in Paris**. But if you have some reason why you must rent a car and drive yourself there are a few things you need to know:

The roads in France are classified into 5 types, they're numbered and begin with letters: *A* (autoroute, expressways), *N* (route nationale), *D* (route départmentale), and the smaller *C* or *V*.

There are lots of great connections between Paris and most other cities in France. It's best to avoid rush hour times (7-9:30 am and then 4:30-7:30 pm).

Outside Ile-de-France, you have to pay toll (péage) to drive on most of the expressways. The rates vary and can be expensive. Some allow you to pay with your credit card.

Gas is pretty expensive in the city. Most gas stations are located in underground tunnels or large parking garages. If you're driving outside of Paris, it's best to wait until you get outside the city limits to fill your gas tank.

Boat Travel

Batobus. This is our first recommendation. This is run by the city and provides a quiet, commentary-free cruise along the Seine. You can get off and on at various stops along the way. Departure from several locations: Champs-Elysées, Eiffel Tower, Jardin des Plantes, Notre-Dame, Hotel de Ville, St-Germain-des-Pres, Musée d'Orsay. www.batobus.com **Telephone**: 08-25-05-01-01.

Bateaux Mouches. For a leisurely hour-long tour of Paris, take one of these well-known motorboat rides. The ride includes views of the Eiffel Tower and the mini-version of the Statue of Liberty. For current pricing and more information: www.bateaux-mouches.fr **Telephone:** 01-42-25-96-10.

Vedettes du Pont Neuf. You can also take a nice cruise along the famous River Seine, which includes a bi-lingual guide (verses the recorded canned info on the Bateaux Mouches).
www.vedettesdupontneuf.com

Telephone: 01-46-33-98-38.

• Tours •

Is time limited? Don't speak French? Why not try a **guided tour?** Paris can be overwhelming for first or even second-timers, so this could be a great option for enhancing your trip in pleasantly unexpected ways!

Before booking a tour, it's important to know what's included and what's not for the price, which may not always include taxes and fees, so be sure to telephone or visit the websites to find out. You should also be prepared to **tip the tour guide** in cash when the tour's over.

By Bike

You can take an organized bicycle tour in and around Paris with a number of companies. The guides always speak English and the cost always includes a **bike and helmet.** Tours start at around €30. It's best to make a reservation.

We recommend **Fat Tire Bike Tours**. This tour is great! They offer a nighttime bike trip that includes a riverboat cruise on the Seine.

Contact Info: 24 rue Edgar Faure, 15e, Paris, 75015. **Tel:** 01-56-58-10-54; 866-614-6218 from the U.S and Canada. www.fattirebiketoursparis.com.

By Boat

Boat tours are also a great way to see the city, for first-timers and return travelers alike. There are several companies that sightsee along the Seine. Boat tours typically take anywhere from 1-2 hours.

We recommend the **Batobus** or **Canauxrama**. Prices start at about €15.

Contact Info:

Batobus | Port de la Bourdonnais, 7e, Paris, 75007. 08-25-05-01-01. www.batobus.com.

Canauxrama| 13 Quai de la Loire, 19e, Paris, 75019. 01-42-39-15-00. www.canauxrama.com.

By Bus

For a great bus tour with headsets that give you an informative commentary in a variety of languages, and special recordings for the kids, we recommend **Paris City Vision**. Tickets start at €20.

Contact Info: 2 rue des Pyramides, Paris, 75001 | **Tel:** +33144556100 www.pariscityvision.com

We can also recommend:

Paris L'OpenTour| 13 rue Auber, 9e, Paris, 75009 | **Tel:** 01-42-66-56-56. www.parislopentour.com

Les Cars Rouge| 17 Quai de Grenelle, 15e, Paris, 75015 | **Tel:** 01-53-95-39-53. www.carsrouges.com

By Minibus or Car

You can also opt for a minibus, car or limousine tour of Paris. We recommend **Paris Major Limousine**, **Paris Trip**, or **Paris City Vision**. Minibus tours are great for large families, friends, or social groups. Price can range from €75 to €500.

Contact Info:

Paris Major Limousine | 199 bld. Malesherbes, 17e, Paris, 75017 | **Tel:** 01-44-52-50-00. www.1st-limousine-services.com

Paris Trip | 2 Cité de Pusy, 17e, Paris, 75017 | **Tel:** 01-56-79-05-23. www.paris-trip.com

Paris City Vision | 2 rue des Pyramides, Paris, 75001 | www.pariscityvision.com

Try Special Interest or Walking Tours

Love to shop? Check out **Chic Shopping Paris!** Visit their website for tour packages tailored to your shopping interests. Tours start at about €100. **Tel:** 09-77-19-77-85 | **US Office:** 573-355-9777.
 www.chicshoppingparis.com

Love food? **Paris by Mouth** offers delicious tasting tours by local food writers. They can also include wine tasting, baguette-making and other specialties.
www.parisbymouth.com

Would you like some help navigating the museums? Try **Paris Muse**! They have English-speaking **art historians** on staff who. Pricing includes admission to museum and ranges from €80 to €280. **Tel:** 06-73-77-33-52. www.parismuse.com

If you'd like an intimate tour of the city, we recommend **Context Paris**. They take you on fabulous and detailed tours of Paris's art culture and architectural history. Prices range from €70 per person for a 2½-hour group tour to €550 per party for a full day of custom touring (up to five people). **Tel:** 09-75-18-04-15 | **US Office:** 800-691- 6036. www.contexttravel.com

We also recommend **Secrets of Paris** for personally tailored daylong or half-day walking tours through Paris neighborhoods. **Tel:** 01-71-20-42-27 | www.secretsofparis.com

For a well-rounded engagement of the city, we highly recommend **Black Paris Tours.** They offer an amazing exploration of the city locales made famous by people of color — artists, writers, musicians, etc. Visit the website for pricing and reservations! **Tel:** 01-46-37-03-96 | **US Office:** 972-325-8516. www.blackparistour.com

There are also volunteers who'll take you on a walking tour free of charge, called **Paris Greeters (Parisien d'un Jour)**. You get a much more personal look at life in Paris for people who live there. Although it's free, donations are welcome. www.parisgreeters.fr

• 5 Days In Paris! •

Enjoy this 5-day itinerary for a well-balanced, easy-going Parisian experience! Modify or adjust if you like!

• Day 1 •

Once you arrive at your hotel (or wherever you're staying) relax a bit, get settled and then freshen up before venturing out to explore the surrounding area. A walk or cruise along the bridges of the **River Seine** is always nice; or perhaps if you're up for it, go ahead and see the Eiffel Tower or the Arc de Triomphe? For the **Eiffel Tower**, it's best to buy tickets online and print them in advance to avoid the long lines. **For Arc de Triomphe**, be prepared to climb lots of stairs, but it's worth it!

If you can, **lunch at a nearby bistro** and **have dinner in an elegant restaurant** before heading back to the hotel for a good night's rest so you're refreshed and renewed, ready to dive into your second day in the city!

• **Eiffel Tower Tickets:**
http://www.toureiffel.paris/en/preparing-your-visit/buying-your-tickets.html

• Day 2 •

You may choose to have breakfast at your hotel or at a nearby cafe. Then get yourself over to the **Latin Quarter** in the 5th and 6th arrondissement, on the left bank of the Seine, and explore the distinct atmosphere of this neighborhood. You can arrange for a guided walking tour (Discover Walks: www.discoverwalks.com/paris-walking-tours/left-bank-tour) or you can opt to go wherever the wind blows you.

Be sure not to miss the **Luxembourg Gardens**—they're beautiful!

The Jardin du Luxembourg
6e Arrondissement, 75006 Paris, France
www.senat.fr/visite/jardin/index.html

We suggest **lunch at Allard** (41 rue Saint-André des Arts, www.restaurant-allard.fr) an authentic French restaurant nestled in the Latin Quarter.

After lunch, head over to visit **Notre Dame Cathedral**, or to the **Panthéon** if historic gothic churches aren't really your thing. Both are nearby.

• **Notre Dame** is free Monday - Friday 8:00am to 6:45pm and 8:00am to 7:15pm on weekends. To go up the towers the cost as of this writing is €8.50.

• From April to September the **Panthéon** is open 10:00am - 6:30pm. From October to March they close at 6:00pm.

And to cap off the day, enjoy some nightlife on the **Rue de la Huchette**—a street with lots of places to eat, drink and dance the night away before catching the train back to your hotel, or splurging on a cab if you'd like.

• Day 3 •

How about a full **day-trip** to visit Louis XIV's **Château de Versailles?** It's only a short ride from Paris on the suburban train to Versailles. Buy your tickets in advance to avoid the long lines and make sure you get there when they open at 9:00 am, there's lots of ground to cover! Be sure to bring a **bottle of water, snacks and sunscreen.** You may also want to carry a light sweater, as Versailles is cooler than Paris.

There are a variety of ways to experience the Chateau, so take your pick and enjoy! (http://billetterie.chateauversailles.fr/index-css5-chateauversailles-lgen-pg1.html) If you have a Paris Museum Pass (http://en.parismuseumpass.com/) you'll be admitted without charge but may need to purchase a garden ticket. **Garden tickets** are additional on Tuesdays, Saturdays and Sundays, and on exceptional dates during the peak season.

The Chateau's gardens and groves are not to be missed and we recommend renting a golf cart for a more enhanced tour than you get on foot.

There's a food market on the way to the Palace when you leave the train station so you can have a nice **picnic for lunch,** or you can have a nice dine-in lunch at La

Flottille (http://www.laflottille.fr), which is located in the gardens.

When you get back to your hotel, you can freshen up and go out for dinner in a nearby restaurant, or just order in room service if the day's been long enough.

• Day 4 •

Take a morning stroll through **Le Marais** in the 3rd and 4th arrondissement on the right bank of the Seine (Rive Droite). Once a swamp and historically Paris's Jewish quarter, today it's a trendy upscale neighborhood full of arts and crafts. Spend some good time in the many lovely parks and gardens.

After lunch, (hopefully you've already purchased tickets!) head over to the Louvre and visit Mona Lisa. (http://www.louvre.fr). Located in the 1st arrondissement. If there are specific things you want to see, try to make a loose agenda, as **the Louvre is huge** and you may run out of time if you just stroll aimlessly. Also think about bringing along bottled water and light snacks.

The most common entrance is the glass pyramid in the courtyard but this can be very high traffic with long lines. We recommend entering in the Carrousel du Louvre, the underground shopping mall with the inverted pyramid, next to an Apple store.

You can have dinner in any number of cafes and restaurants located in the museum. Many have indoor and outdoor seating.

Louvre Museum: 75001 Paris, France • **Tel:** +33 1 40 20 50 50. Please check the website for the most current hours of operation and plan accordingly. (http://www.louvre.fr/en/hours-admission)

• Day 5 •

In the morning, head over to the **Montmartre** area in the 18th arrondissement and enjoy a stroll through one of Paris' most historic neighborhoods! Take pictures on the steps of the world-famous **Basilique du Sacré-Coeur** then have your very own portrait made in the **Place du Tertre**. You can even visit the Moulin Rouge!

You can **have a nice lunch** while in the Montmartre at the infamous **Café des 2 Moulins**, one of our favorite bistros in the neighborhood. (**Address:** 15 Rue Lepic, 75018 Paris, France • **Tel:** +33 1 42 54 90 50)

Spend the rest of your day however you'd like — if there's time, try cruising along the Seine, or visiting another museum or must-see spot that you had in mind; or you could just rent a bicycle and explore the city at your own pace. There are several local bike rental companies to choose from — we recommend **Paris Bike Tour**. (13 rue Brantôme, 75003, Paris, France • **Tel:** 01 42 74 22 14) Check the website for current rates. (http://parisbiketour.net/bike-rental-paris).

Now may be a great time to check out one of our recommended spots for **Luxury or Bargain Eats!**

• Best Places For Travelers on a Budget •

Since Paris is well known for being one of the most expensive cities in Europe, you may be surprised to know there are inexpensive places to stay — you just have to know where to look!

With proper planning, you can explore the **budget-friendly options** that are available. Sleeping in economical historic mansions, filling up on gourmet cuisine and freewheeling along the Seine can be a lot less costly than you imagined.

Bargain Sleeps

Accommodations are usually your biggest daily expense when on vacation so it's crucial to choose your neighborhood, as rates vary depending on where you choose to stay. The areas near tourist attractions like the Champs-Élysées or Eiffel Tower are often too costly for smaller budgets, but there are some exceptions.

Check the websites for current rates:

Hôtel Monte Carlo for instance is an affordable option in the 9th arrondissement. **Address:** 44 Rue du Faubourg Montmartre, 75009 Paris, France • **Tel:** +33 1 47 70 36 75 • www.hotelmontecarlo.fr

• How to get to Hotel Monte Carlo?
Metro 7: Le Peletier

Metro 8 and 9: Grands Boulevards
Metro 12: Notre Dame de Lorette

Hôtel Esméralda, which is located on a quiet street in the 5th arrondissement, is budget-friendly and has prime views of Notre Dame Cathedral. **Address:** 4 Rue Saint-Julien le Pauvre, 75005 Paris, France • **Tel:** +33 1 43 54 19 20 • www.hotel-esmeralda.fr

• How to get to Hôtel Esméralda?
RER Station B: St. Michel-Notre Dame
Metro 4: St. Michael

Hôtel Vic Eiffel is a great little boutique hotel in the 15th arrondissement, with the Eiffel Tower just a stroll away. **Address:** 92 Boulevard Garibaldi, 75015 Paris, France • **Tel:** +33 1 53 86 83 83 • http://www.hotelviceiffel.com/en

• How to get to Hôtel Vic Eiffel?
Take metro line 6 towards Charles-de-Gaulle-Étoile and get off at Sèvres-Lecourbe

In the 11th arrondissement, **Hôtel Beaumarchais** offers relatively low non-refundable rates when you book online, not uncommon among many Parisian hotels. **Address:** 3 Rue Oberkampf, 75011 Paris, France • **Tel:** +33 1 53 36 86 86 •
http://www.hotelbeaumarchais.com

• How to get to Hôtel Beaumarchais?
Metro line to le Marais

Cosmos Hôtel is just footsteps from the rue Jean-Pierre Timbaud's great Parisian nightlife. Also in the 11th arrondissement. **Address:** 35 Rue Jean-Pierre Timbaud, 75011 Paris, France • **Tel:** +33 1 43 57 25 88 • http://www.cosmos-hotel-paris.com

• How to get to Cosmos Hôtel?
Metro Access: Parmentier - République RER Access: Station Gare Du Nord

It is important to reiterate here that it's actually rare to get a single hotel room in Paris. The ones you do find are equal to the cost of a double.

The larger establishments like the modern hostel **St. Christopher's Inn** in the 10th arrondissement, serve guests affordable evening meals, rent bicycles and organize excursions. **Address:** 5 Rue de Dunkerque, 75010 Paris, France • **Tel:** +33 1 70 08 52 22 • http://www.st-christophers.co.uk/paris-hostels/gare-du-nord

• How to get to St. Christopher's Inn?
Metro line 5 to Gare Du Nord

Another top-choice is the 18th arrondissement's **Plug-Inn Hostel at Montmartre,** a cute boutique hostel that has a kitchen where guests can cook their own meals. **Address:** 7 Rue Aristide Bruant, 75018 Paris, France • **Tel:** +33 1 42 58 42 58 • http://plug-inn.fr

• How to get to Plug-Inn Hostel at Montmartre?
Metro line 2 to Blanche

Bargain Eats

In Paris, eating well can become as costly as your lodging expenses, but it doesn't *always* have to blow your budget. In restaurants and bistros, you can save by ordering the "**plat du jour**" (dish of the day), which is often a less expensive option than ordering á la carte.

Also, ordering a **jug of water** during or after your meal is often cheaper than buying bottled water.

Another trick to spending less on food in Paris, is in having a heavier lunch and grabbing a lighter picnic-type dinner later, since lunch options tend to cost a lot less than dinner.

You should also try to **avoid the restaurants and bistros** near major sightseeing spots, as their prices tend to be tourist-influenced = expensive.

Marché des Enfants Rouges is the oldest covered farmer's market in Paris and a wonderful place that sells various **ready-to-eat dishes** in food stalls. (**Address:** 39 Rue de Bretagne in the Marais (3rd) arrondissement. Closed on Mondays.)

Wine bars like **Les Pipos** in the 5th arrondissement (**Address:** 2 Rue de l'École Polytechnique, 75005 Paris, France • Tel: +33 1 43 54 11 40), or **Le Zinc des Cavistes** in the 9th (**Address:** 5 Rue du Faubourg Montmartre, 75009 Paris, France • **Tel:** +33 1 47 70 88 64) are very good low-cost options.

• Best Spots for Ultimate Luxury in Paris •

If you're looking for the absolute best places to stay and dine while in Paris, look no further. We've got three fabulous high-end recommendations that are guaranteed to exceed your loftiest expectations. Relax and enjoy!

Luxury Parisian Sleeps

The new and amazing **Maison Souquet** is a recently opened 5-star hotel in the 9th arrondissement (opened March 2015), located just a stone's throw from the famous Moulin Rouge, and it's also within walking distance of the Montmartre area. You can enjoy a special drink made by an ultra chic 'mixologist' when you check in! **Address:** 10 Rue de Bruxelles, 75009 Paris, France • **Tel:** +33 9 75 18 64 25 • www.maisonsouquet.com

A wonderful hotel for the traveling family is **Bel-Ami Hotel** in the St. Germain neighborhood, 6th arrondissement. Although located in a quieter area of Paris, it manages to be central to most of the popular sites! **Address:** 7-11 rue Saint Benoit | 6th Arr., 75006 Paris, France • **Tel:** +33 1 42 61 53 53 • www.hotelbelami-paris.com

Really into luxurious design and decor? **Le Royal Monceau-Raffles Paris** is a visual feast and seasoned in the trendy and polished Parisian lifestyle.

8th arrondissement. **Address:** 37 Avenue Hoche, 75008 Paris, France • **Tel:** +33 1 42 99 88 00 • www.leroyalmonceau.com

Luxury Parisian Eats

For the finest dining in Paris, we can't recommend the following three restaurants highly enough. Three standout gems on the French culinary scene, you're guaranteed to leave desperate to be back for more!

For classic high-end French fare, book a reservation at the fabulous **L'Epicure.** You'll need to plan ahead for sure on this spot, like months in advance. It's that popular. It's that good. 8th arrondissement. **Address:** 112 Rue du Faubourg Saint-Honoré, 75008 Paris, France • **Tel:** +33 1 53 43 43 40

Perhaps you feel like high-end Italian while in France? Well, the very charming and cozy **Ristorante Lo Spaghettino** is your spot. Located in the Opera/Bourse neighborhood in the 9th arrondissement, it's a pretty small restaurant, so you do need to plan ahead and make a reservation. The cuisine is most delish! **Address:** 7 Rue Geoffroy-Marie, 75009 Paris, France • **Tel:** +33 1 53 34 62 87

If you're looking for a dynamite steak and beer in Paris, book a table at the **Publisher.** This pub-style restaurant is also famous for wonderful English-style cuisine. So definitely try the fish and chips — delicious! 8th arrondissement. **Address:** 33 rue de Constantinople, 75008 Paris, France • **Tel:** +33 9 84 01 74 47

• Paris Nightlife •

Apart from the reputation that Paris has for fine food, art, history and classic beauty, the city also offers a wonderfully diverse nightlife! You can enjoy everything from hard rock to opera to throbbing nightclubs and intimate bars.

Tickets for all kinds of shows and concerts can be bought at **FNAC Forum des Halles** (**Address:** 1/7 rue Pierre Lescot, 75001, Paris France • **Tel:** +33 825 02 00 20)

Great Bars in Paris

We have three fabulous recommendations:

L'Ave Maria: This is an interesting bar to have a drink in while in the city. Unlike the many kitsch-style bars in Paris, L'Ave Maria has a great blend of substance and style. Their menu includes Brazilian fare, and the cocktails are awesome, but not extortionate. The music policy is très cool. Cash only. **Address:** 1 rue Jacquard, 75011, Paris, France, 11th arrondissement. **Tel:** +33 1 47 00 61 73.

Café Charbon: This Parisian café is located in a restored Belle Époque structure and has become the center of the thriving Rue Oberkampf nightlife. The Charbon also has an advantage in that it's located next to the Nouveau Casino, a very energetic nightclub you won't be able to miss. Explore! **Address:** 109 Rue Oberkampf, 75011, Paris, France, 11th arrondissement. **Tel:** +33 1 43 57 55 13.

Melac: For a traditional Paris bar experience, complete with zinc bar tops, well-chosen wines and cheeses, visit Melac! **Address:** 42 Rue Léon Frot, 75011 Paris, France, 11th arrondissement. **Tel:** +33 1 43 70 59 27 • http://www.melac.fr

Great Clubs in Paris

Two great recommendations:

La Perle is a cool Parisian club that usually has a nice blend of straight and gay clubbers who are equally well dressed. Parisian hedonism, which is done the old way, is the theme. **Address:** 78 Rue Vieille du Temple, 75003, Paris, France, 3rd arrondissement. **Tel:** +33 1 42 72 69 93.

Rex Club plays a heavy mix of dance and techno music with an ever-changing musical line up that keeps the experience fresh! Not necessarily a spot for the budget-conscious, but the Rex Club experience is well worth it. **Address:** 5 Boulevard Poissonnière, 75002 Paris, France, 2nd arrondissement. **Tel:** +33 1 42 36 10 96 • http://www.rexclub.com

Great Live Music in Paris

Any or all of these recommendations are well worth seeing if you love live bands!

Caveau de la Huchette has played jazz for over 60 years. Listen, dance and enjoy the fun! **Address:** 5 Rue de la Huchette, 75005 Paris, France, 5th arrondissement. **Tel:** +33 1 43 26 65 05 • http://www.caveaudelahuchette.fr

Nouveau Casino is a hot Parisian club, which is next to the aforementioned, Café Charbon, that hosts live nightly concerts and DJs perform afterwards so you can dance the night away. **Address:** 109 Rue Oberkampf, 75011 Paris, France, 11th arrondissement. **Tel:** +33 1 43 57 57 40 • http://www.nouveaucasino.net

Point Éphémère is a converted warehouse that has studios for professional and amateur dancers. It also has art workshops, exhibition spaces and creative conferences. **Address:** 200 Quai de Valmy, 75010 Paris, France, 10th arrondissement. **Tel:** +33 1 40 34 02 48 • http://www.pointephemere.org

Great Theatre in Paris

Comédie Française is one of the most famous theatres in the world and is renowned for its classic productions. Some say an evening here is a lifetime experience! **Address:** 1 Place Colette, 75001 Paris, France, 1st arrondissement. **Tel:** +33 825 10 16 80 • http://www.comedie-francaise.fr

Théâtre de la Ville shows the works of some of the high-profile choreographers, such as Maguy Marin, Karine Saporta and Pina Bausch. **Address:** 2 Place du Châtelet, 75004 Paris, France, 4th arrondissement. **Tel:** +33 1 42 74 22 77 • http://www.theatredelaville-paris.com

The theatre also has another venue with the same contact details at 31 rue des Abbesses, 18th arrondissement.

Great Music and Dance

We have two amazing recommendations for amazingly produced performances! Everyone knows about the Moulin Rouge, but also take in a show at one of these great venues:

The Opéra National de Paris offers phenomenal ballet and opera performances at the **Opéra Garnier** (**Address:** 8 Rue Scribe, 75009 Paris, France, 9th arrondissement • **Tel:** +33 1 71 25 24 23 • http://www.operadeparis.fr)

Châtelet Théâtre Musical de Paris has a great ambiance, super comfortable seats and excellent productions. (**Address:** 1 Place du Châtelet, 75001 Paris, France, 1st arrondissement • **Tel:** +33 1 40 28 28 28 • http://chatelet-theatre.com)

• Conclusion •

We hope you've found our guide to the beautiful city of Paris helpful and wish you a safe, happy and fun-filled trip to France!

Warm regards,

The Passport to European Travel Guides Team

Visit our Blog! Grab more of our signature guides for all your travel needs!

http://www.passporttoeuropeantravelguides.blogspot.com

★ **Join our mailing list** ★ to follow our Travel Guide Series. You will be automatically entered for a chance to win a **$100 Visa Gift Card** in our monthly drawings! Be sure to respond to the confirmation e-mail to complete the subscription.

• About the Authors •

Passport to European Travel Guides is an eclectic team of international jet setters who know exactly what travelers and tourists want in a cut-to-the-chase, comprehensive travel guide that suits a wide range of budgets.

Our growing collection of distinguished European travel guides are guaranteed to give first-hand insight to each locale, complete with day-to-day, guided itineraries you won't want to miss!

We want our brand to be your official Passport to European Travel — one you can always count on!

Bon Voyage!

The Passport to European Travel Guides Team
http://www.passporttoeuropeantravelguides.blogspot.com

Manufactured by Amazon.ca
Bolton, ON

32108177R00033